TO TURNER,

WITH BEST WISHES,

M. D. BECCACECI

29/4/96.

PatagoniaWilderness

Patagonia Wilderness

MARCELO D. BECCACECI
BONNIE J. HAYSKAR

PANGAEA

Saint Paul

INTERNATIONAL STANDARD BOOK NUMBER: 0-9630180-1-9

LIBRARY OF CONGRESS CATALOGUE CARD NUMBER: 91-90541

ALL PHOTOGRAPHY BY MARCELO D. BECCACECI,
EXCEPT THE FOLLOWING PAGES, COURTESY OF:

FLORIAN VON DER FECHT 4, 5, 6, 17, 28, 53, 57, 58
ALEJANDRO E. POPOVICI 79, 91, 95
BONNIE J. HAYSKAR 7, 10, 11, 61, 64, 66 (l)

PUBLISHED BY

P A N G A E A

226 SOUTH WHEELER STREET
SAINT PAUL, MINNESOTA, USA
612/690-1485

PRINTED IN THE UNITED STATES OF AMERICA

FIRST EDITION 1991

To all the Argentine Rangers who,
working hard every day
under frequently adverse conditions,
care for the wilderness of this extraordinary region of our world
for present and future generations.

A todos los Guardaparques y Guardafaunas Argentinos que,
trabajando duro cada día
bajo frecuentes condiciones adversas,
cuidan la prístina naturaleza de esta extraordinaria región de nuestro mundo
para las presentes y futuras generaciones.

CONTENTS

PROTECTED NATURAL AREAS IN PATAGONIA

PATAGONIA
ARGENTINA

MOUNTAINS

STEPPE

COAST

NON-PATAGONIA
ARGENTINA

RESERVA TURISTICA
FORESTAL LAS LAGUNAS

RESERVA PROVINCIAL
DE FAUNA LAGUNA TROMEN

PARQUE PROVINCIAL
COPAHUE CAVIAHUE

NEUQUEN

• Neuquén

RESERVAS FORESTALES
BATEA-MAHUIDA & CHANY

P. N. LAGUNA
BLANCA

P. N. LANIN

P. N. LOS ARRAYANES
• Bariloche
& NAHUEL HUAPI

RIO NEGRO

• Viedma

RESERVA TURISTICA
PROVINCIAL PUNTA
BERMEJA

COMPLEJO
ISLOTE LOBOS

PARQUE MARINO
PROVINCIAL GOLFO SAN JOSE

PENINSULA VALDES

P. N. LAGO PUELO

P. N. LOS ALERCES

• Esquel

Trelew •
Rawson •

RESERVA FAUNISTICA
PROVINCIAL ISLA ESCONDIDO

RESERVA FAUNISTICA
PROVINCIAL PUNTA TOMBO

RESERVA FAUNISTICA
PROVINCIAL PUNTA ROJA

RESERVA FAUNISTICA
PROVINCIAL CABO DOS BAHIAS

CHUBUT

BOSQUES PETRICADOS
JOSE ORMAECHEA &
VICTOR SZALEPSIS

• Comodoro Rivadavia

RESERVA NATURAL
CABO BLANCO

P. N. PERITO
MORENO

RESERVA NATURAL
RIA DESEADO

MONUMENTO NATURAL
BOSQUES PETRIFICADOS

SANTA
CRUZ

P. N. LOS
GLACIARES

• Calafate

RESERVA PROVINCIAL
ISLA DE LOS PINGUINOS

Rio Gallegos •

Strait of
Magellan

TIERRA DEL
FUEGO

P. N. TIERRA
DEL FUEGO
• Ushuaia

ISLA DE LOS
ESTADOS

Beagle
Channel

South Pacific Ocean

CHILE

PATAGONIA

South
Atlantic
Ocean

SOUTH
AMERICA

ARGENTINA

• Buenos Aires

PROLOGUE

Cast against the vastness of the South American sky, an astonishing panorama of color and form and life reveals itself in the land called Patagonia. From the massive glaciated crags of the Andes Mountains through dense subantarctic forests, across the ancient sea bed that is now the barren steppe, the land drops precipitously to the sea. Everywhere the forces of nature have uniquely shaped this land, its plant life and bountiful animals.

The earth's most southerly landmass above Antarctica and the furthest reach of the Americas, Patagonia lies predominantly in Argentina with a portion in Chile. Because of its remote location, it has been the subject of lore for centuries. A land of often formidable extremes, it has dwarfed man and remained relatively untouched to this day, everywhere providing evolutionary clues in its remnants of petrified forest, volcanoes, glaciers and coastal cliffs layered with fossilized marine life.

Stretching from the edge of the Argentine pampas along the Río Colorado in the north to Tierra del Fuego and the Beagle Channel near Cape Horn in the south, Patagonia ranges eastward from the Andes to the South Atlantic Ocean. Occupying over a quarter of the country, Argentina's Patagonia is 308,000 square miles/800,000 square kilometers, including approximately 1,200 miles/1,920 kilometers of mountain range and 1,100 miles/1,770 kilometers of ocean coast merging at the southern terminus. This volume presents the three distinct geographical divisions of Argentine Patagonia: mountains, steppe and coast.

The Cordillera de los Andes is the longest continuous mountain range on earth. Its serpentine expanse stretches from one end of South America to the other, some 4,500 miles/7,245 kilometers from the north to its abrupt retreat at the tip of Tierra del Fuego. Argentina alone has 29 peaks over 20,000 feet/6,096 meters, the highest range outside Asia, and includes Aconcagua's 22,834 feet/6,960 meters, the highest in the western hemisphere. It is these magnificent mountains that so profoundly influence Patagonia's nature.

Scientists estimate that nearly 175 million years ago the earth was comprised of one supercontinent, from which our present-day world derives. That continent has been named Pangaea and surrounding the giant landmass, anchored to Antarctica, was one universal sea, Panthalassa. The theory of continental drift of the Jurassic period, which accounted for the massive movement of the earth's last great reconfiguration, was advanced by Alfred Wegener in 1912 and the resultant concept of plate tectonics is now widely accepted. It attributes the formation of the continents to the shifting of the earth's crust on a molten subterranean sea variously splitting open, sinking and rising.

It was over 100 million years ago that South America drifted away from Antarctica and existed in total isolation until a land bridge to Central America arose, the residue of volcanic eruptions. What is today regarded as the "Ring of Fire," a circle of volcanic activity extending around the entire Pacific Ocean, was to give birth to the Andes twenty million years ago. The fertile land that had risen from the sea during the previous era, now fell dormant in the rain shadow cast by the giant peaks. The rains that had fallen so richly on the land were stolen. Petrified trees, preserved by the volcanic ash, lie where the lush araucaria forests grew. And the once verdant plains of Patagonia now swirl with dust in its fallow river beds, only a half dozen major waterways making their way from the mountains to the sea.

Valleys of frozen rain from the last Ice Age that followed the volcanoes persist today. Patagonia's subantarctic icecap extends over 23,000 square miles/59.570 square kilometers and supports 47 different glaciers, many of which are hundreds of feet deep. Surprisingly, one continues to advance. Their spectacular beauty is evident throughout the Patagonian Andes. Close to the mountains, melting glaciers release rainwater trapped for millenia and feed deep, clear alpine lakes and rivers carved by glacial retreat. There, too, are rare primeval forests and meadows of wildflowers.

The steppe, on the parched side of the Andes and extending to the coast, developed its own arid beauty. It is patched with grasses and bushy scrub that nurture a wonderful array of mammals and birds, including the gentle guanaco and the rhea.

Like Madagascar and Australia, South America was isolated for millions of years and was to evolve differently from the rest of the world. Animals that would early on become extinct elsewhere, continue to thrive in Argentina, with the armadillo and mara retaining their places in Patagonia to this day. Many of the region's birds and animals are considered endangered or threatened by the International Union for the Conservation of Nature and Natural Resources (IUCN), the international body that establishes the Red List of species nearing extinction.

Nowhere is the richness of Patagonia's animal life more evident than where it meets the sea. Punta Tombo has the second largest penguin rookery in the world, after Antarctica, hosting a million Magellanic penguins during the breeding season. The southern right whales return to the Patagonia coast each year, along with southern sea lions, elephant seals and fur seals on the shore. From throughout the South Atlantic they journey to this safe harbor.

The Spanish explorer Ferdinand Magellan and his crew are credited with naming Patagonia in 1520 while grounded en route to the Pacific Ocean. While the exact details have taken on the character of legend, it is believed that upon seeing the large footprints of the Indian moccasins, which were in all probability made from the hides of guanaco, they proclaimed the region the land of the big feet, Patagonia.

Many of the Indian tribes--Tehuelche, Haush, Ona, Yaghan, Alacaluf, and Mapuche-- are all but gone today. Their numbers were never great in Patagonia, estimated to have totalled only about 10,000 in pre-colonial times, prior to the mid-sixteenth century. It was one of the last areas on earth to experience human habitation. Today, Patagonia remains sparsely populated, despite its wealth of natural phenomenon.

The Argentine and provincial governments of Neuquén, Río Negro, Chubut, Santa Cruz and Tierra del Fuego, however, have long recognized the significance of Patagonia. The first national park in South America, Parque Nacional Nahuel Huapi, was founded there in 1904. It was one of the first national parks in the world. The lands were donated by Francisco "Perito" Moreno, a pioneer in the preservation of the environment. The system of parks and reserves is extensive and provides an opportunity to view Argentina's many unusual animals, birds and plants in dramatically varying landscapes, including many endangered species.

This book was created to characterize Argentina's Patagonia, in the hopes that with familiarity will come understanding and appreciation, both vital to assure the future protection of its wilderness.

PatagoniaWilderness

2

The granite Macizo (Massif) Fitz Roy (11,073 feet/3,375 meters) and the aiguille of Cerro Torre (10,256 feet/3,126 meters), Parque Nacional Los Glaciares, rise above glacial footholds that reach back to the Pleistocene, vestiges of the last Ice Age.

I
MOUNTAINS

The spectacle of the snow-capped Cordillera de los Andes rising from the plain calls to mind the forming of the earth. The giant rift that split the surface in volcanic eruption was encased in ice millions of years later. That period of glaciation and the living process of glacial formation, are visible throughout the Patagonian Andes, most prominently at Parque Nacional Los Glaciares.

It is the extraordinary height of the mountains there that contributes to the persistence of the glacial process. With a constant supply of moisture from the atmosphere, the snows of the Andes at high elevation form thick layers of ice that accumulate faster than they melt. The sheer weight of the snows compact to form a dense mass called *névé* or *neviza*. Pressure continues to force air molecules out until the substance is clear and hard, known as a *geloide*. It is the bluish crystalline *geloide* that flows down the valleys, pressing and scraping the granite escarpments that contain it. It spills out from the bowls and extends as far as it can before dissipating in a warmer environment.

While most of the earth's glaciers have been in regression since the end of the Ice Age, there are a few that continue to advance due to the peculiarities of their location and the surrounding climatic and atmospheric conditions. Patagonia is an area where these conditions exist within the same region as volcanoes to the north at Parque Nacional Lanín--truly a land of fire and ice. Left behind, in the lower reaches of the mountains are the

deep glacial lakes and streams of Bariloche's lake district and, to the south, Parque Nacional Los Alerces where some of the oldest living trees on earth stand.

These mountains and forests create a habitat for creatures unlike anywhere else. Patagonia's two native deer, the elusive pudú, the world's tiniest deer, inhabits the thick cane forests and the huemul lives above the treeline. Everywhere the land and waters are alive with bird life both common and uncommon from the magnificent Andean condor, the largest land bird in existence to the southernmost parakeets and hummingbirds.

The Andes range comprises the entire western border of Argentina. From its greatest height in the north, with peaks over 20,000 feet/6,096 meters, the mountains gradually decrease in size until they round Tierra del Fuego to the east and slip into the chill waters of the Beagle Channel and South Atlantic Ocean.

There on the islands of Tierra del Fuego, the mountains take on the character of dense cold rainforests. Scientists suggest that it was one of the last land masses to break away from Antarctica and lose its glaciers. The land may be less than 10,000 years old. One hundred mile-per-hour winds off the Antarctic icecap frequently lash its forests of lenga, coihue and other southern beeches, which huddle at the base of the mountains and on the lower slopes in yet another unusual ecosystem in the mountains of Patagonia.

The "monkey puzzle tree" (left) is an araucaria or pehuén that can grow to nearly 150 feet/45 meters with a complex of stiff leaves about its branches, hence the name. This mature tree has shed its lower limbs and resembles a giant parasol. It is a primitive conifer of ancient derivation, discernible in the petrified woods of Patagonia and its fossils. The bark shingles off from a trunk that can reach up to 6.7 feet/2 meters in diameter. The large seeds of the tree remain a food source for the Mapuche Indians of the region. The araucaria grows in moist, cold regions at elevations of 2,950 feet/900 meters to 5,900 feet/1,800 meters. The largest of these trees is believed to be more than a thousand years old.

Volcan Lanín (12,383 feet/3,774 meters), Parque Nacional Lanín (facing page), is perpetually snow-capped. The park is a forest preserve for pehuén or araucaria; raulí that can grow to 50 feet/15 meters with atypical beech leaves of four to five inches in diameter; and roble pellín. All are species found only in this area of Argentina.

Pudú and huemul deer live here, along with the southern river otter or huillín. They are considered to be threatened species.

Parque Nacional Nahuel Huapi is one of the few places in the world where one can see arrayán trees en masse. Within the park, Isla Victoria and Península Quetrihué have areas specifically set aside to protect them. The peninsula was established as a separate national park (Parque Nacional Los Arrayanes) in recognition of the tree's eminence, an inviolate natural monument.

The trees were immortalized in the Walt Disney film, *Bambi*, when a scouting crew decided on this rare and colorful forest as the backdrop to the classic animated film. Its distinctive pale orange bark curls into parchment-like scrolls on strangely contorted trunks, giving the pure stands of arrayanes a mystical effect.

The trees produce bright white blossoms in the spring (right); and tiny blue-black edible fruits in the fall.

Lago Nahuel Huapi, Parque Nacional Nahuel Huapi (facing page), is the largest of the Patagonian glacial lakes carved during the Pleistocene. Its surface covers 215 square miles/557 square kilometers and it is 60 miles/97 kilometers long at its widest point. The park, with typically Andean-Patagonian vegetation, runs from the highest point of the continental divide to the edge of the steppe, encompassing a wide variety of terrain. Its waters flow to both the Atlantic and Pacific oceans.

Tronador (Thunderer) is the highest peak in the park at 11,722 feet/3,573 meters. As its glaciers calve and slide down the mountainside, it sounds like a distant storm.

Cerro Catedral (Cathedral Hill) is a 7,000-foot/2,134-meter ridge of spire-like pinnacles that resembles a granite church.

The austral thrush (right) is a typical bird of the araucano forest. It is also found in nearby areas and villages of Patagonia.

Parque Nacional Los Alerces was established to protect the ancient larch trees. Sometimes referred to as the sequoias of South America, the enormous conifers may exceed 150 feet/46 meters and have more than a 12-foot/3.7-meter diameter. They are some of the oldest living things on earth, with one tree in the park estimated to be about 2,600 years old. It stands over 200 feet/61 meters tall.

The mountains in the park are in the range of 7,900 feet/2,400 meters above sea level and surround the clear glacial lakes and rivers. Four endangered species inhabit the area: pudú, huemul, south Andean cat or huiña, and Chilean pigeon.

9

The route from the north to Parque Nacional Los Alerces is predominated by cypresses, a coniferous tree that grows in the transitional zone between steppe and mountain.

Lago Rivadavia (right), at the northern edge of Parque Nacional Los Alerces, is surrounded by snowcapped mountains and glacial fields. It is one of several long, meandering lakes in the park that in spring and summer are rimmed with woodland wildflowers.

The coligue cane (facing page), a form of cold rainforest vegetation related to the bamboo, grows midway up the park's mountain slopes. The tall canes are solid rather than hollow and grow to 3-23 feet/ 1-7 meters. The dense growth conceals the delicate pudú, a small deer less than 15 inches/ 38 centimeters at the shoulder. The cane is shown here in bloom, which occurs only once in its life after approximately nine years of growth. It drops its seed and dies shortly thereafter.

11

Río Arrayanes (above and facing page), Parque Nacional Los Alerces, links Lago Futalaufquen to Lago Verde.

The 2-mile/3.22-kilometer stretch is lined with arrayanes that display abundant white blooms in late February/early March .

The Andes chain from the top of Cerro Alto del Dedal (6,286 feet/1,916 meters), Parque Nacional Los Alerces, extends far beyond the horizon.

The black-chested buzzard eagle is one of the largest birds of prey in Patagonia. It glides high over open spaces and is found throughout Argentina. Shown on this page is a young eagle.

The adult black-chested buzzard eagle bears a black shield on its chest and is also known as a "shielded eagle."

Cerro Fitz Roy, Parque Nacional Los Glaciares, is among the most difficult in the world to scale, along with nearby icecapped Cerro Torre.

The pinnacles of Fitz Roy emerge sharply from the flat plain with only meager foothills. The effect is striking viewed from the steppe.

Enshrouded in an ever-changing veil of mist, Cerro Fitz Roy has been called *Chaltén* by the Indians, meaning "Blue Peak."

The Andean condor reigns over the Andes, soaring at great heights that diminish its size. Its wingspan can reach nearly 10 feet/3 meters. Its distinctive white collar and wing patch are easily discernible. The condor is a glider and its outstretched primaries at the tips of its wings resemble open fingers.

The red cascade flower known as "stream tears" is always found near small cascades or waterfalls. An herbal perennial, it blooms in the spring producing elongated bell-shaped flowers about a half-inch/1.5 centimeters long.

The mountain paths are scattered with hundreds of varieties of alpine wildflowers throughout the spring and summer months and into the fall.

Glaciar Piedras Blancas is one of the smaller glaciers in the Fitz Roy area, Parque Nacional Los Glaciares.

Río de las Vueltas is the northern border of Parque Nacional Los Glaciares and flows from the mountains to Lago Viedma.

The Magellanic woodpecker is the largest in South America and one of the largest in the world. The female, shown here, has a black hood with curled crest and red face, while the male has a red hood. They live in the araucano forest and are up to 14.4 inches/37 centimeters in overall length.

Glaciar Perito Moreno, Parque Nacional Los Glaciares, is one of the most fascinating in the world and one of the few that is still advancing. Its sheer scale and mass are accessible for viewing as it makes its way 22 miles/35 kilometers through the Andes to Lago Argentino. The face of the glacier is about three miles/4.8 kilometers wide with a sheer headwall that rises nearly 200 feet/60 meters above the surface of the water at Canal de los Témpanos (Iceberg Channel).

In 1944 Glaciar Moreno crossed the lake and collided with Cerro Buenos Aires at Península Magallanes, forming a glacial dam that cut off two arms of Argentino, Brazo Rico and Brazo Sur. These dammed-up areas continued to receive water , rising 100 feet/300 meters above the water level of Lago Argentino. By 1947, water had begun to seep through the glacial ice and formed a tunnel, which eventually collapsed, releasing a flood of water that thundered through the channel and out into the main lake.

The inexorable advance of Glaciar Moreno continues and the cycle of advance and collapse repeats itself approximately every four years. During the intervening times, great blocks of ice break away from the glacier crashing to the lake producing high waves and forming icebergs, set adrift on the lake.

Parque Nacional Los Glaciares is located between 48 and 51 degrees southern latitude and is covered by a portion of the Patagonic continental ice sheet that runs 560 miles/902 kilometers south to north and 25-38 miles/40-61 kilometers west to east, approximately 23,000 square miles/59,570 square kilometers. The park contains thirteen glaciers that flow into the Atlantic Ocean. UNESCO declared it a World Heritage Site in 1981.

The surface of Glaciar Moreno is approximately 75 square miles/195 square kilometers in size, fed by smaller glaciers that surround it.

Throughout the day, great pillars of ice slip from the headwall of the glacier and collapse with the sound of thunder to the lake surface below. The enormous pieces of ice appear to fall in slow motion due to their size and the crack of the ice as it expands in the valley resonates for great distances. Glaciar Perito Moreno is regarded as one of the most significant natural wonders in the world.

The deep-throated flower of the notro (right) is particularly attractive to hummingbirds who sip its nectar. The bark and leaves have medicinal qualities and the woody parts are used for furniture.

The notro (facing page) usually stands alone in a clearing and does not form groves. Frequently resembling a bush when immature, it can grow to heights of 20 feet/6 meters. It blooms during spring and early summer, holding its leaves all year.

Glaciar Perito Moreno is in an evergreen area of lenga, coihue and canelo trees, with the glacial-swept Andes as a backdrop..

The reflective quality of Glaciar Moreno ice responds dramatically to the changing light (above, facing page and next two pages).

Glacial moraines form distinctive dark sedementary fissures in the ice as debris is carried away as the glacier carves its path.

39

The crystalline ice of Glaciar Perito Moreno is the characteristic blue of glaciers and causes the same aqua blue to appear in Lago Argentino where it melts, discharging its glacial rock flour.

Glaciar Upsala (above) is the largest glacier in the park, 30 miles/50 kilometers long and 6 miles/10 kilometers wide.

Three glaciers converge at Lago Onelli (facing page): Agassiz, Bolado and Onelli.

Brazo Rico (above) is an extension of Lago Argentino periodically flooded when closed off by the advancing Glaciar Moreno.

Throughout Tierra del Fuego, including Isla de los Estados, there are mountains with marshes and peatlands in the valleys beside lakes and woodlands. The extensive peat bogs (facing page) develop in flooded areas where partially decayed debris is prevented from decomposing by the cold, acidic waters. It is on this base that layers of spaghnum moss, lichens and rushes develop.

There are also grasslands on Isla Grande (left), the largest island in Tierra del Fuego.

In 1520, Magellan and his crew had named the area Tierra del Fuego, "Land of Fire," because of the many fires visible from the ship, presumably lit by the Alacalufes as signals. Magellan was on a voyage to the Pacific-- Peaceful Sea-- which he called it, having escaped the turbulent waters off Tierra del Fuego.

Springtime sees the return of the ashy-headed goose (left) to Patagonia. It is always near araucano forests and wetlands, in woodland clearings or near the shores of lakes and rivers.

The subantarctic rainforest of Parque Nacional Tierra del Fuego (next two pages) includes the large southern beech trees lenga, coihue and ñire. The forest canopy is thick with interlocking branches, in part to conserve rainfall but also to protect itself from the powerful winds that sweep this land, regularly reaching 100miles/160 kilometers per hour. Due to the poor soil and cold climate, trees may take 70- 100 years to mature.

45

47

49

The great-horned owl (facing page) inhabits the forests of Patagonia and can be found in many different landscapes.

The red fox (above) is the largest land predator in Tierra del Fuego. This native fox is quite large, about as tall as a medium-sized dog.

Río Chubut forms an important oasis in the arid steppe.

II
STEPPE

Reading the chronicle *The Voyage of the Beagle* a century and a half after naturalist Charles Darwin made his journey with Captain Robert Fitz Roy, one is struck by the descriptions of Patagonia still visible today. "The plains of Patagonia are boundless, for they are scarcely passsable, and hence unknown: they bear the stamp of having lasted, as they are now, for ages, and there appears no limit to their duration through future time."

Darwin remained intrigued by the steppe upon his return to England: "Why then, and the case is not peculiar to myself, have these arid wastes taken so firm a hold on my memory?" The stereotypical vision of the Patagonian steppe as a vast lifeless expanse of windswept desert belies the richness of this peculiar ecosystem for as Darwin knew, it is the product of extraordinary geological and biological epochs.

Quite literally an ocean floor that rose some 200-300 feet/660-990 meters above sea level, it had experienced this rise and fall many times in its past, each time accumulating the shells of bygone eras, now visible to several hundred feet/meters in depth and rising like giant platforms from the coast to the cordillera.

Its ancient history includes the remains of prehistoric animals, barely concealed by the surface gravel, and littered with the petrified remains of ancient forests. Many of the animals that inhabit these plains are throwbacks to creatures extinct in the rest of the world.

The once lush land is parched. While a handful of rivers still drain the run-off from mountains and glaciers, many beds are but dried remnants of the past. The grasslands for the most part have disappeared and bushy scrubland predominates. An indigenous tree is rare.

In this dry and muted land, strange and unusual creatures have evolved, including flightless birds such as the lesser rhea and near flightless tinamou. Herds of graceful guanaco run freely on the plain and the occasional mara or Patagonian hare scampers away. What appears to be a stillife landscape comes vividly alive the longer one observes it.

The coloration of the resultant jagged and rounded landforms runs from rich chocolate brown to orange to soft gray, taking on golden illumination with the Patagonian sunrise and sunset. Small tufts of desert grasses are sprinkled across the expanse, interspersed with rugged shrubs. Clinging to the earth are a great variety of delicate wildflowers.

All these life-forms have adapted to this seemingly inhospitable environment and render it spellbinding.

Parque Nacional Laguna Blanca is dedicated to the preservation of the black-necked swan (right), a sacred bird to the ancient Tehuelche Indians.

The swans, shown here with a white-winged coot (black with yellow bill) and two silver teals to the right of the swans, is exclusive to the extreme south of South America.

Nesting begins in November when the swans lay four to five eggs; cygnets are most likely to be seen with the adult birds from February through April.

The swan population varies from hundreds to more than 2,000, but the coots number in the thousands nearly year-round.

Parque Nacional Laguna Blanca (facing page) is one of only two reserves in the world set aside specifically to protect swans (the other is for the trumpeter swan, Red Rock Lake National Wildlife Refuge, Montana, United States).

The large, shallow alkaline lake holds no fish. The swans feed on vegetation, including algae, and small arthropods. The area is typical of the pre-cordilleran steppe.

It is at Laguna Blanca where the geological forces of volcanic formation and ancient seabed meet clearly. There are no trees in the park, only spiny shrubs and other plants adapted to extreme drought.

The largest number of birds can be seen in February, including swans, grebes, ducks, gulls, herons, and flamingos on the lake.

The results of the erosionary forces of wind and water that courses through Río Chubut valley are visible in the adjacent landforms.

Río Chubut is one of the most important rivers in Patagonia. The only places with trees on the steppe are along the few remaining rivers.

The guanacos run freely on the steppe. Speed is their only defense against their main predator, the puma.

Guanacos, related to the llamas, are the largest of the land vertebrates in Patagonia. They have been highly prized by man for their coats, especially the heavy winter covering shown here nearly shed in springtime.

They are gregarious animals, living in groups with a territorial male, up to ten females and their young. The erect stature and steady gaze of the guanaco exemplify the defiant spirit of Patagonia.

57

58

The young guanacos (this page) stay with the herd until they attain maturity, at which time the male yearlings (facing page), known as *chulengos*, are expelled. They form a separate herd, occasionally challenging the solitary male to master the females.

The guanaco is found throughout the steppe and to elevations of 16,000 feet/5,570 meters. Its favorite food is *coirón*, a common grass.

The puma is the largest predator in Patagonia.   Often found in the transition zone of steppe to mountain, it is the enemy of the guanaco.

The steppe grasses grow in a variety of shapes and colors, complementing the rich textures of the landscape.

The lesser rheas or *choiques* (right) are Patagonia's largest running birds and related to the pampas' greater rheas. They form large groups and scatter rapidly when frightened. Several females lay their eggs, frequently more than thirty, in a single nest. The male incubates the eggs and cares for the chicks, called *charitos*, until self-reliant.

They are well adapted to the steppe, surviving with little water and feeding on insects, small rodents, other bird chicks and plant matter.

The mara (facing page) is a curious animal. The endemic rodent is large, reaching about two feet as an adult, and hops much like a kangaroo. It has the body of a rabbit, but small ears.

A member of the family *Caviidae,* maras are related to capybaras and guinea pigs.

Maras excavate burrows in the steppe under shrubs and give birth to their young, typically two babies, which remain in the burrow for several weeks. Sometimes a nursery of sorts is formed with an adult female looking after the young.

A little armadillo (right) exclusive
to the region, the Patagonian piche
is one of the early primitive
animals in Argentina.

Argentina's four large petrified forests (facing page) and smaller
reserves are all in Patagonia and considered to be some of the best
in the world. The most extensive is Monumento Natural Bosques
Petrificados (Petrified Forests Natural Monument), 25,000
acres/10,000 hectares in size.

The state of preservation of the Argentine petrified forests and the
size of the specimens are significant. Petrified trees in the United
States and Australia, for example, measure less than six feet/1.8
meters in diameter while many of the araucaria trees of Argentina
are in excess of ten feet/three meters in diameter and 90 feet/27
meters long.

The volcanic ash that covered the early forests, many millions of
years ago after the formation of the Andes, killed the trees but
preserved them from decay. The pressure of the tons of ash turned
the wood to stone over time, fossilized.

65

According to legend, if you eat the calafate berry, you will return to Patagonia. The sweet purple fruit follows bright yellow blossoms on the box-leaved barberry. Common throughout Patagonia, the calafate berry was used by Indians to paint themselves and for cave drawings.

A bird common throughout Patagonia, the rufous-collared sparrow is the tamest bird in the region. It is one of four sparrows found in Argentina.

Upland geese enjoy areas of
Patagonia with waterways,
woodlands, meadows and
marshes. This male is in a moist
zone with tender grasses,
known as a *mallín* by local
people. They join migratory
flocks of ashy-headed and
ruddy-headed geese in winter.

The upland goose nests on the
ground, laying eight creamy
eggs, cared for by both male and
female.

67

While benefitting from the mountains and their glacial run-off, Lago Argentino is on the steppe. The lake is about 600 feet/185 meters above sea level with a surface area of 600 square miles/1,560 square kilometers.

Due to its composition of glacial runoff, the lake is a spectacular aqua blue to green set in the arid plain. The lake was formed by advancing and receding glaciers about 60 miles/100 kilometers further east. Lago Argentino flows into Río Santa Cruz, ending in the South Atlantic Ocean.

Lago Argentino (above) hosts a variety of bird life, including the Chilean flamingo.

The Chilean flamingo is one of three species of flamingo in Argentino. They feed on plankton, fly in flocks and breed in colonies..

The Península Valdés coast rises in steep-walled cliffs above the South Atlantic Ocean, rimmed with colonies of wildlife.

III

COAST

The land that rose from the sea along Patagonia's eastern edge millions of years ago now nurtures remarkable marine life in its sheltering waters and on its shore. The flat steppe extends its jagged ledge over 1,000 miles/1,600 kilometers along the South Atlantic Ocean.

The waters there combine the warm ocean current of Brazil to the north with the cold current from Islas Malvinas (Falkland Islands) to create an underwater world of unusual diversity. The seas hold vast amounts of plankton, algae, crustaceans and fish, food for one of the largest breeding areas for marine life on earth, as well as myriad species of sea birds.

The coast, particularly along Península Valdés, has protected waters in its gulfs and inlets, to which these birds and animals return year after year to mate and raise their young. It is one of the most important wildlife areas in the world.

Southern elephant seals, found only in the southern hemisphere, breed exclusively on Península Valdés in the South Atlantic and on the Indian Ocean coast. Other families of marine mammals, including the southern sea lions and southern fur seals, number in the hundreds and colonies of them stretch for mile upon mile of beach.

The largest of the marine mammals, the southern right whale, returns to the coast each year to breed in its calm waters before returning to the high seas. Designated a threatened species, they are abundant along the coast of Península Valdés in its gulfs from May to December. They share these waters with orcas, also known as killer whales, and dolphins.

Most abundant, however, are the Magellanic penguins that number nearly a million. At Punto Tombo, a narrow peninsula 6 miles/10 kilometers long, the remarkable sight of the enormous penguin colony stretches as far as the eye can see. There are other colonies at Punta Roja, Cabo dos Bahías, Puerto Deseado, Cabo Vírgenes, Caleta Valdés, and San Lorenzo.

Other species of birds drawn to the sea live along the cliffs and in areas near the coast, including the rare Chubut steamer duck, a flightless bird that lives only along the Chubut province coast of Patagonia.

The fossilized shells from a pre-historic Atlantic are as many as several hundred feet deep along the coast, remnants of yet other extraordinary ages where Patagonia begins.

At the base of the cliff along the Patagonian coast, the southern sea lion returns each year to breed and nurse its offspring.

Adult male sea lions migrate to the rookeries in December to establish their territory and gather their mates. The male and female (left) stay together until conception, at which time the female goes to the sea for a twelve-month gestation period. She returns to the rookery to give birth to one pup each year from the time the female reachs maturity at age five to about age twelve.

The southern sea lion derives its name from the appearance of the adult male. When seen in profile its thick. coarse hair that surrounds its face and broad neck resembles a lion's mane.

The full-grown adult male, or bull, can weigh twice as much as the female , or cow. Males can mature to 660-1100 pounds/300-500 kilograms with a length of over eight feet/2.5 meters.

The male establishes a harem and is extremely proprietary of his territory. He may go as much as two months without food during the active breeding period to assure that other males do not attempt to mate with his females, which may number as many as fifteen.

The sea lions form large colonies of breeding and nursing units, with the unpaired males forming bachelor colonies. Hundreds of sea lions will participate in the colonies, which are found along the coast of Península Valdés and other areas.

The old male sea lion (above) lives a solitary life. The males are dark while the females (facing page) are lighter.

Young sea lion pups are nursed on the land for up to a year.

When only a few months old, the pups waddle about on the beach and soon begin their swimming lessons, gathering in groups of up to 200, in waters protected by the offshore reef.

Between March and May is a dangerous time for the young sea lions, for their chief predator the orca, or killer whale, visits the rookeries. It swims offshore, awaiting the high tide that can carry it close to its prey. The orca has been known to throw itself onto the shore to capture the young pups, then to be swept back to sea by the waves.

Valued for its pelt, the once prolific southern fur seal (facing page) was hunted relentlessly in the nineteenth century and is now a threatened species in Argentina. It exists only in small colonies along the southernmost shores of Patagonia.

The primary difference between sea lions and fur seals is that the fur seals have thick underfur. This underfur was prized for garments and led to the animal's near extinction.

79

80

The largest seals on earth, the southern elephant seals can grow to 21 feet/6.4 meters and weigh nearly 9,000 pounds/4,050 kilograms. While the female is less than half that size, she still bears a pup each year that averages 90 pounds/40 kilograms (facing page and above).

The highest rate of birth takes place in October. Two weeks later the female, or cow, will conceive again. The pup will be nursed for a relatively short period (20 to 25 days on average) before the female returns to the sea.

The elephant seal bulls, much like the sea lions, arrive at the pebble beaches in advance of the females to establish their territories, gathering their harem as the females return. One male may gather as many as forty females, showing aggression toward any males that attempt to enter his territory or approach his females.

The female can bear her first young at three years of age, with the average gestation period of almost a year.

The young elephant seals (right) nurse for less than a month. The cow's milk is rich in fat, nearly fifty percent, and the pups gain weight quickly, preparing them for the cold of the ocean life they are to begin. The lactation takes its toll on the mothers, however, who lose weight rapidly during this time. They abandon their pups and return to the males to conceive once again, then take to the ocean to recover.

The pups are left completely alone when lactation ceases. The adult males leave the beach, followed by the females and eventually, after two to four weeks, the young join them. Throughout their lives, their main predators are the orca, white shark and Antarctic leopard seal.

The estimated annual elephant seal population on Península Valdés is 15,000, making it the largest in the Americas.

The elephant seal takes its name from the large, inflatable, trunk-like snout of the male, shown here with a female.

Only approximately 3,000 southern right whales survive, making them a threatened species in the world today. A significant group of about 450 of these breed in the waters of Golfo Nuevo and Golfo San José along Península Valdés, an established sanctuary. They have been declared a Natural Monument in 1984 by the Argentine government, the first species to receive this designation providing absolute protection within Argentine jurisdiction.

The giants of the sea have a length of about 45 feet/14 meters and can weight as much as 50 tons/4,500 kilograms. They roam the open seas for the first half of the year, seeking the shelter of the Patagonian waters from June to December to breed and raise their young.

During the breeding season, the female will copulate with several males each day . She will return to the same waters the following year to bear her calf. The female right whale calves only once every three years.

Mother and calf stay together for the first two to three months after birth becoming accustomed to one another and learning to swim closely together before heading out to sea.

The whales can be seen playing and pursuing one another near to the shore, either in courtship or rearing their young. By December, the beginning of the austral summer, the southern right whales return to the open Atlantic to feed on the vast storehouses of plankton that emerge at that time.

85

The skin of the southern right whale is generally grayish black with irregular patterned areas on the ventral and dorsal sides. A white calloused spot on its large head is unique to each whale and a means of identification for scientists tracking them.

The right whale, a sea mammal, must surface every few minutes to breath. After surfacing, it frequently gives a characteristic flap of its enormous v-shaped tail before descending.

This white southern right whale is unusual in its coloration and rarely seen.

90

Punto Tombo hosts the largest colony of Magellanic penguins on the South Atlantic coast. It numbers as many as one million annually.

The Magellanic penguins spend nearly half a year in the South Atlantic Ocean before returning to the Patagonian coast. Major penguin rookeries, or *pingüineras*, are located near Península Valdés at Punto Tombo, a thin stretch of land that juts six miles into the sea, and at Cabo Dos Bahías, as well as other areas along the coast.

The male arrives ahead of the female to repair the nest, generally one which has been previously excavated by the couple at the base of a shrub or on the open ground.

In early September, the females arrive and an elaborate courtship begins with much noisemaking and posturing.

The female will lay the first white egg soon afterwards; a second will follow in three to four days. Incubation is shared by both parents and lasts about 40 days. In early November the two chicks will be born.

Both parents feed the young penguin chicks by regurgitation. The chicks live under the protection of their parents' bodies for several days after birth, each parent taking turns on the nest while the other forages for food.

The penguin parents are fearless in the protection of their young against numerous predators that feed on eggs and chicks alike: skuas, southern giant petrels and gulls.

For three months the brooding will continue until the chicks are able to forage on their own. By February or March they are learning to swim.

Immature penguins born the previous year return to the colony to molt their feathers in November. The mature adults molt in March and April, leaving the colony with their young, not to return until the next year.

They will travel the seas north to southern Brazil and south in subantarctic waters.

Pictured above is a family with three chicks, which is unusual. Typically penguins only produce two offspring each season.

The Magellanic penguins share the parenting of their young (above) until they all take to the ocean in the austral fall (facing page).

Kelp and dolphin gulls prey on penguin offspring (above). The kelp gull, shown with chicks (facing page), is common in Argentina.

The blackish oystercatcher is usually found on the rocky shores of Patagonia in pairs or small groups up to six. It feeds on marine mollusks and is a typical coastal bird of the area.

Nesting on the ground, it lays two to three spotted eggs. In winter, it migrates north.

The dolphin gull is prolific along the southern tip of Patagonia. It nests in colonies in the coastal areas. It is relatively tame and may, therefore, seem aggressive.

The snowy sheatbill originates in Antarctica and is also found in Patagonia. It lives in groups, frequently in sea mammal colonies, nesting among the rocks and in hollows. Basically a terrestrial bird, it does little flying and appears rather tame.

Like the gulls, the South American tern exists along a broad range of coast in the southern part of Argentina during the warm months, traveling to the north during the winter.

While considered a sea bird, the tern does not actually swim; it plunges from the sky to takes its prey and then flies off. It enjoys the company of fellow terns and lives in colonies on the coast.

100

In Patagonia, the Chilean flamingo is found on lakes, but also on the coast at Península Valdés and Isla de los Pájaros (Bird's Island).

The Chubut steamer duck shown here incubating her nest (facing page), is a flightless bird that lives only along the Chubut coast.

An elegant bird, the rock cormorant has a long, rigid tail and long neck extended in flight. It nests on vertical rock walls in colonies.

Unlike the rock cormorant, the blue-eyed cormorant (above) is also found on inland waters. It, too, is an excellent diver.

Tierra del Fuego, set at the southernmost tip of South America and divided between Argentina and Chile, is a large archipelago of thousands of islands. Isla Grande (left) is the largest, separated from the mainland by the Strait of Magellan, ending at Cape Horn where the Atlantic and Pacific oceans meet.

Parque Nacional Tierra del Fuego is the southernmost national park in the world. Its sheltered waters are rich with marine life, including pinnipeds (seals) and sea birds.

105

The flightless steamer duck
(right) is one of the three species
of steamer ducks that, along
with two species of rhea and
various species of penguin,
constitute the flightless birds of
Argentina.

A large duck, weighing up to 14
pounds/6 kilograms, it churns
across the water flapping its
wings in a rapid circular motion
resembling a paddlewheel boat
or steamer, for which it was
named.

Near the Beagle Channel coast in Parque Nacional Tierra del Fuego, the last of the Andean cordillera peaks are visible.

Multiple species co-exist along the Beagle Channel coast, including blue-eyed cormorants and southern sea lions (above and facing page).

The kelp goose lives exclusively on the coast of Tierra del Fuego. It feeds on the large kelp seaweed that abounds in the Fuegian sea. It winters further north.

The male is white with orange beak and legs; the female is dark and well camouflaged for the rocky areas it inhabits. The kelp geese pictured (right) include the male, female and chicks on an island in the Beagle Channel.

SCIENTIFIC NAMES

For fauna and flora pictured in book

BIRDS

Andean condor. *Vultur gryphus.*
ashy-headed goose. *Cloephaga poliocephala.*
austral thrush. *Turdus falcklandii.*
black-chested buzzard eagle. *Geranoaetus melanoleucus.*
blackish oystercatcher. *Haematopus ater.*
black-necked swan. *Cygnus melancoryphus.*
blue-eyed cormorant. *Phalacrocorax atriceps.*
Chilean flamingo. *Phoenicopterus chilensis.*
Chubut steamer duck. *Tachyeres leucocephalus.*
dolphin gull. *Leucophaeus scoresbii.*
flightless steamer duck. *Tachyeres pteneres.*
great-horned owl. *Bubo virginianus.*
kelp goose. *Cloephaga hybrida.*
kelp gull. *Larus dominicanus.*

lesser rhea. *Pterocnemia pennata.*
Magellanic penguin. *Spheniscus magellanicus.*
Magellanic woodpecker. *Campephilus magellanicus.*
rock cormorant. *Phalacrocorax magellanicus.*
rufous-collared sparrow. *Zonotrichia capensis.*
silver teal. *Anas versicolor.*
snowy sheatbill. *Chionis alba.*
South American tern. *Sterna hirundinacea.*
upland goose. *Cloephaga picta.*
white-winged coot. *Fulica leocoptera.*

MAMMALS

guanaco. *Lama guanicoe.*
mara. *Dolichotis patagonum.*
Patagonian piche. *Zaedyus pichyi.*

puma. *Felis concolor.*
red fox. *Dusicyon culpaeus.*
southern elephant seal. *Mirounga leonina.*
southern fur seal. *Arctocephalus australis.*
southern right whale. *Eubalaena australis.*
southern sea lion. *Otaria flavescens.*

FLORA

araucaria. *Araucaria araucana.*
arrayán. *Myrceugenella apiculata.*
calafate. *Berberis sp.*
coligue. *Chusquea culeou.*
cypress. *Austrocedrus chilensis.*
lenga. *Nothofagus pumilio.*
notro. *Embothrium coccineum.*
stream tear. *Ourisia alpina.*

RESOURCES

READING

Andrews, Michael A. *The Flight of the Condor.* Boston: Little, Brown and Company, 1982.

Ball, Deirdre, ed. *Insight Guides Argentina.* Singapore: APA Publications, 1990.

Box, Ben, ed. *The South American Handbook 1991.* London: Trade and Travel Publications, 1990.

Bridges, E. Lucas. *Uttermost Part of the Earth: Indians of Tierra del Fuego.* 1949. New York: Dutton, 1988.

Chatwin, Bruce. *In Patagonia.* New York: Summit Books, 1977.

Daciuk, Juan. *La Fauna del Parque Nacional Laguna Blanca.* Buenos Aires: Anales de Parques Nacionales, tomo XI, 1966.

Darwin, Charles. *The Voyage of the Beagle.* 1836. New York: New American Library, 1972 .

Dimitri, Milan. *Aspectos fiteogeográficos del Parque Nacional Lanín.* Buenos Aires: Anales de Parques Nacionales, tomo VIII, 1969.

_____. *Pequeña Flora ilustrada de los Parques Nacionales Andino-Patagónicos.* Buenos Aires: Anales de Parques Nacionales, tomo XIII, 1974.

Dorst, Jean. *South and Central America: A Natural History.* New York: Random House, 1967.

Durrell, Gerald. *The Whispering Land.* London: Penguin Books, 1964.

Erize, F. *Los Parques Nacionales de la Argentina.* Buenos Aires: Incafo, 1981.

González, Alberto Rex and José A. Pérez. *Argentina Indigena: Vísperas de la conquista.* Buenos Aires: Editorial Paidos, 1987.

Goodall, Natalie P. *Tierra del Fuego.* Buenos Aires: Ediciones Shanamaum, 1979.

Hargreaves, Clare, ed. *Backpacking in Chile and Argentina.* Bucks, England: Bradt Publications, 1991.

Hudson, W. H. *Idle Days in Patagonia.* London: Everyman's Library, 1984.

International Union for the Conservation of Nature and Natural Resources (IUCN). *Conservar el Patrimonio Natural de América Latina y del Caribe.* Morges, Switzerland: IUCN, 1961.

-----. *1962 United Nations List of National Parks and Protected Areas.* Morges, Switzerland: IUCN, 1962.

Leitch, William C. *South America's National Parks.* Seattle: The Mountaineers, 1990.

Leitner, G. *Travel Companion Argentina.* Mudgeeraba, Queensland, Australia: Travel Companion, 1990.

Luna, H. C. *La Conservación de la Naturaleza: Parques Nacionales Argentinos.* Buenos Aires: Servicio Nacional de Parques Nacionales, 1976.

Matthiessen, Peter. *The Cloud Forest.* New York: Viking Press, 1961.

Morrison, Tony. *The Andes.* New York: Time-Life Books, 1975.

Narosky, Tito and Darío Yzurieta. *Birds of Argentina and Uruguay.* Buenos Aires: Vazquez Mazzini Editores, 1989.

Oficina Regional de la FAO para América Latina y el Caribe. *Sistemas nacionales de Areas Silvestres Protegidas en América Latina.* Santiago: 1988.

Perry, Roger. *Patagonia: Windswept Land of the South.* New York: Dodd, Mead, 1974.

Theroux, Paul. *The Old Patagonian Express.* Boston: Houghton Mifflin Company, 1979.

INFORMATION

Secretaría de Turismo de la Nación
Suipacha 1111
(1368) Buenos Aires, Argentina
Tel. (1) 313-6220

Offices of Argentina Secretariat of Tourism:

12 West 56th Street, New York, NY 10019 USA

3550 Wilshire Blvd., Suite 1459,
Los Angeles, CA 90010 USA

Via B. Ammannati 6, 00197 Rome, Italy

Adenaueralle 52, 5300 Bonn 1, Germany

Servicio Nacional de Parques Nacionales
Avenida Santa Fe 690
(1059) Buenos Aires, Argentina

INDEX

PATAGONIA WILDERNESS

DESIGNED BY PANGAEA.

CREATED ON A COMMODORE AMIGA 2000 COMPUTER WITH PAGESTREAM 2 SYSTEM,
ASSISTED BY BRADFORD C. RICHTER, ARTEMAGE.

COMPOSED IN PALATINO, WITH DISPLAY LINES IN CASLON, AND
PRODUCED ON LINOTRONIC 530 BY BOB'S LITHO, INC.;
WITH COLOR SEPARATIONS AND FILM ASSEMBLY BY SLY LITHO, INC.

PRINTED ON A HEIDELBERG PRESS
AT LITHO SPECIALTIES, INC.
ON NORTHWEST PAPER COMPANY/POTLATCH CORPORATION'S
QUINTESSENCE REMARQUE, A RECYCLED PAPER.

BOUND IN SKIVERTEX SENEGAL
BY MIDWEST EDITIONS, INC.